# A
# CHRISTMAS
# ALBUM

# A CHRISTMAS ALBUM

Compiled by Sam Elder

GOOD WISHES

I send you
the same
old greeting
tendered
Year by Year,
A happy
Christmas
and a bright
New Year

**HARPER & ROW, PUBLISHERS, New York**

Cambridge, Philadelphia, San Francisco,

1817    London, Mexico City, Sao Paulo, Sydney

Compilation copyright © 1986 Sam Elder

First published in Great Britain by
Orbis Book Publishing Corporation Ltd, London
A BPCC plc company

Designer: Martin Bronkhorst

FIRST EDITION

**Library of Congress Cataloging-in-Publication Data**

Main entry under title:
A Christmas Album.
1. Christmas – Miscellanea. I. Elder, Sam.
GT4985.C3848   1986   394.2′68282   86-45093
ISBN 0-06-015557-4

Printed in Hong Kong

# CONTENTS

# CHRISTMAS IS A-COMING

O you merry, merry souls
Christmas is a-coming,
We shall have flowing bowls,
Dancing, piping, drumming.

Delicate minced pies,
To feast every virgin,
Capon and goose likewise,
Brawn, and a dish of sturgeon.

Then, for your Christmas box,
Sweet plum cakes and money,
Delicate Holland smocks,
Kisses sweet as honey.

Hey for the Christmas Ball,
Where we shall be jolly,
Coupling short and tall,
Kate, Dick, Ralph and Molly.

Then to the hop we'll go,
Where we'll jig and caper,
Cuckolds all a-row,
Will shall pay the scraper.

Hodge shall dance with Prue,
Keeping time with kisses,
We'll have a jovial crew
Of sweet smirking Misses.

*Anonymous, 18th century*

# THE CAROL SINGERS VISIT JOSEPH'S FARM

We approached our last house high up on the hill, the place of Joseph the farmer. For him we had chosen a special carol, which was about the other Joseph, so that we always felt that singing it added a spicy cheek to the night. The last stretch of country to reach his farm was perhaps the most difficult of all. In these rough bare lanes, open to all winds, sheep were buried and wagons lost. Huddled together, we tramped in one another's footsteps, powdered snow blew into our screwed-up eyes, the candles burnt low, some blew out altogether, and we talked loudly above the gale.

Crossing, at last, the frozen mill-stream – whose wheel in summer still turned a barren mechanism – we climbed up to Joseph's farm. Sheltered by trees, warm on its bed of snow, it seemed always to be like this. As always it was late; as always this was our final call. The snow had a fine crust upon it, and the old trees sparkled like tinsel.

We grouped ourselves round the farmhouse porch. The sky cleared, and broad streams of stars ran down over the valley and away to Wales. On Slad's white slopes, seen through the black sticks of its woods, some red lamps still burned in the windows.

Everything was quiet; everywhere there was the faint crackling silence of the winter night. We started singing, and we were all moved by the words and the sudden trueness of our voices. Pure, very clear, and breathless we sang:

> As Joseph was a walking
> He heard an angel sing;
> 'This night shall be the birth-time
> Of Christ the Heavenly King.
>
> He neither shall be bornèd
> In Housen nor in hall,
> Nor in a place of paradise
> But in an ox's stall. . . .'

And two thousand Christmases became real to us then; the houses, the halls, the places of paradise had all been visited; the stars were bright to guide the Kings through the snow; and across the farmyard we could hear the beasts in their stalls. We were given roast apples and hot mince-pies, in our nostrils were spices like myrrh, and in our wooden box, as we headed back for the village, there were golden gifts for all.

*Laurie Lee*

# PATAPAN

Willie, take your little drum,
 With your whistle, Robin, come!
When we hear the fife and drum,
*Tu-re-lu-re-lu, pat-a-pat-a-pan,*
When we hear the fife and drum,
Christmas should be frolicsome.

Thus the men of olden days
Loved the King of kings to praise:
When they hear the fife and drum,
*Tu-re-lu-re-lu, pat-a-pat-a-pan,*
When they hear the fife and drum,
Sure our children won't be dumb!

God and man are now become
More at one than fife and drum.
When you hear the fife and drum,
*Tu-re-lu-re-lu, pat-a-pat-a-pan,*
When you hear the fife and drum,
Dance, and make the village hum.

*Burgundian carol*
*Translated by Percy Dearmer*

Buone Feste

# THE OXEN

Christmas Eve, and twelve of the clock.
'Now they are all on their knees,'
An elder said as we sat in a flock
By the embers in hearthside ease.

We pictured the meek mild creatures where
They dwelt in their strawy pen,
Nor did it occur to one of us there
To doubt they were kneeling then.

So fair a fancy few would weave
In these years! Yet, I feel,
If someone said on Christmas Eve,
'Come; see the oxen kneel

'In the lonely barton by yonder coomb
Our childhood used to know,'
I should go with him in the gloom,
Hoping it might be so.

*Thomas Hardy*

# CHRISTMAS IN NEW YORK

It was not a white Christmas, to be sure, dulled as it was to a sort of coastal, oyster gray. But in certain spots of the city, something shimmered, if only briefly. For many, the day was bright.

'It's spiritually beautiful,' said Lascell Johnson as he sat down to a chicken dinner prepared by the Salvation Army and served to more than 400 people on West 125th Street. 'It's a good Christmas blessing,' he said, 'another day you can step into the future without giving up.'

For 80-year-old Mariam Anderson, who lives in a nursing home on Staten Island, the opportunity came to telephone her sister in Kristiansand, Norway. She had never done that before, though they exchange visits and letters.

Merrill Lynch, Pierce, Fenner & Smith had brought nearly a thousand elderly people to its headquarters on lower Broadway with an invitation to call anywhere in the world, free. 'She said there was a lot of snow, bitter cold,' Mrs Anderson reported. . . .

Fifth Avenue was jammed and crosstown traffic choked in the 50s. 'Swing Street,' as 52nd Street is now officially designated, was at a standstill because of the heavy traffic. Outside the International Building at Rockefeller Center, a small crowd watched a fire-eater performing under the statue of Atlas, to the accompaniment of the bells of St Patrick's playing 'Come, All Ye Faithful' and 'The First Noel'.

Horse-drawn carriages formed a line in front of the Rockefeller Center Promenade on Fifth Avenue, and beyond them was a ragtag barricade of food vendors. One of them, a young woman from Astoria, Queens, said that, in spite of the crowds, the chestnuts were not moving very briskly. 'There are more pushcarts than people,' she said.

Behind them, in the Channel Gardens, families grouped and regrouped, moving around in bundled clusters, trying to get pictures taken with the enormous Christmas tree as backdrop while avoiding intrusion in someone else's frame.

'It's something out of the ordinary,' said Cosmas LeGrand, who had come with relatives from Brooklyn. 'There's a very family type of atmosphere today.'

*David W. Dunlap,*
*The New York Times,*
*26 December 1981*

# THE HOLLY

The sturdiest of forest-trees
With acorns is inset;
Wan white blossoms the elder brings
To fruit as black as jet;
But O, in all green English woods
Is aught so fair to view
As the sleek, sharp, dark-leaved holly tree
And its berries burning through?

Towers the ash; and dazzling green
The larch her tassels wears;
Wondrous sweet are the clots of may
The tangled hawthorn bears;
But O, in heath or meadow or wold
Springs aught beneath the blue
As brisk and trim as a holly-tree bole
With its berries burning through?

When hither, thither, falls the snow,
And blazes small the frost,
Naked amid the winter stars
The elm's vast boughs are tossed;
But O, of all that summer showed
What now to winter's true
As the prickle-beribbed dark holly tree,
With its berries burning through!

*Walter de la Mare*

17

# A WORD ABOUT WINTER

Now the frost is on the pane,
Rugs upon the floor again,
Now the screens are in the cellar,
Now the student cons the speller,
Lengthy summer noon is gone,
Twilight treads the heels of dawn,
Round-eyed sun is now a squinter,
Tiptoe breeze a panting sprinter,
Every cloud a blizzard hinter,
Squirrel on the snow a printer,
Rain spout sprouteth icy splinter,
Willy-nilly, this is winter.

Summer-swollen doorjambs settle,
Ponds and puddles turn to metal,
Skater whoops in frisky fettle,
Golf-club stingeth like a nettle,
Radiator sings like kettle,
Hearth is Popocatepetl.

Runneth nose and chappeth lip,
Draft evadeth weather strip,
Doctor wrestleth with grippe
In never-ending rivalship.
Rosebush droops in garden shoddy,
Blood is cold and thin in body,
Weary postman dreams of toddy,
Head before the hearth grows noddy.

On the hearth the embers gleam,
Glowing like a maiden's dream,
Now the apple and the oak
Paint the sky with chimney smoke,
Husband now, without disgrace,
Dumps ash trays in the fireplace.

*Ogden Nash*

# GLORIOUS PLUM PUDDING

In a household where there are five or six children, the eldest not above ten or eleven, the making of the pudding is indeed an event. It is thought of days, if not weeks, before. To be allowed to share in the noble work, is a prize for young ambition. . . . Lo! the lid is raised, curiosity stands on tip-toe, eyes sparkle with anticipation, little hands are clapped in extasy, almost too great to find expression in words. 'The hour arrives – the moment wished and feared;' – wished, oh! how intensely; feared, not in the event, but lest envious fate should not allow it to be an event, and mar the glorious concoction in its very birth.

And then when it is dished, when all fears of this kind are over, when the roast beef has been removed, when the pudding, in all the glory of its own splendour, shines upon the table, how eager is the anticipation of the near delight! How beautifully it steams! How delicious it smells! How round it is! A kiss is round, the horizon is round, the earth is round, the moon is round, the sun and stars and all the host of heaven are round. So is plum pudding.

*The Illustrated London News, December 1848*

# THE VIRGIN MARY

To work a wonder, God would have her shown,
At once a bud, and yet a rose full-blown.

As sunbeams pierce the glass, and streaming in,
No crack or schism leave in the subtle skin:
So the Divine Hand worked, and broke no thread,
But in a mother kept a maiden-head.

The Virgin Mary was (as I have read)
The House of God, by Christ inhabited;
Into the which He entered: but, the door
Once shut, was never to be opened more.

*Robert Herrick*

# Santa's Mailbag

Dear Santa
How do you feel? Please for Christmas could I have a violin
and a treble recorder if it is not to much money.
P.S. You get the violin from Tompshon hall in Stretford.
James Flynn

Dear Santa
I would like a stomper, Star Wars things, R2D2, He-man
and Battle Cat, A big horn, walkie talkies, a big bed time
care bear, Glo-bug, some surprises, some clothes, some
lego. Robert Kay

Dear Father Christmas
When you come to my house could
you bring me lots of toys please.
I think you are lovely! (kiss kiss)
I will leave you out some food and
help yourself from the drinks cupboard. When it is
Christmas I think of preasents, turkey, Christmas
crackers, nuts, films, Jesus, and paper hats. Say hello to
the raindeers for me:
Lots of love, Katharine E. Fisher

Dear Santa Claus
I would like a camera if you could bring me one. I hope you
get around all the houses in time. I think you will. You
usually do. Love, Barry Clark

Dear Father Christmas
I hope you dont see any naughty
children if you od dont give them
any presentnsts I want draw
it paint it and a little care-bear.
Lots of love, Emma Woolley

Dear Father Christmas
For Christmas I would like a Sindy House and a big fluffy
care bear and a Care Bear House and a playhouse and a
disco set and my ears pierced. Love from Sarah, age 5

To Father Christmas
For Christmas I would love to have a big care bear. But
could you tell me where you get all the prensents from? If
you could tell me I would be very very happy. Love from
Helen Cornwell

Dear Father Christmas
Please can I have tractor and a farmyard and a trailer to
put my pigs in. Love, Thomas Bezant

Dear Santa
I have been a good girl this year. Could you bring me these
presents. Raleigh Bianca bike, Sweet heart barbie,
Whams new tape with Freedom on it, Duran Durans tape
with the reflex on it, the Barbie pink rara set, the Barbie
Miss World set, the Barbie Spectacular set, the set of
Amelia Jane books by Enid Blyton, the set of Naughtiest
Girl in school books by Enid Blyton, and some stamps.
Love from Vicki Gilritchie

Dear Father Christmas
For Christmas I would like anything. Love from Benjamin

# A Time to Cherish

Some say that ever 'gainst that season comes,
Wherein our Saviour's birth is celebrated,
The bird of dawning singeth all night long;
And then, they say, no spirit can walk abroad;
The nights are wholesome; then no planets strike,
No fairy takes, nor witch hath power to charm,
So hallow'd and so gracious is the time.

*William Shakespeare*

# Preparing for the Day

Gradually there gathered the feeling of expectation. Christmas was coming. In the shed, at nights, a secret candle was burning, a sound of veiled voices was heard. The boys were learning the old mystery play of St George and Beelzebub. Twice a week, by lamplight, there was choir practice in the church, for the learning of old carols Brangwen wanted to hear. The girls went to these practices. Everywhere was a sense of mystery and rousedness. Everybody was preparing for something.

The time came near, the girls were decorating the church, with cold fingers binding holly and fir and yew about the pillars, till a new spirit was in the church, the stone broke out into dark, rich leaf, the arches put forth their buds, and cold flowers rose to blossom in the dim, mystic atmosphere. Ursula must weave mistletoe over the door, and over the screen, and hang a silver dove from a sprig of yew, till dusk came down, and the church was like a grove.

In the cow-shed the boys were blacking their faces for a dress-rehearsal; the turkey hung dead, with opened, speckled wings, in the dairy. The time was come to make pies, in readiness.

The expectation grew more tense. The star was risen into the sky, the songs, the carols were ready to hail it. The star was the sign in the sky. Earth too should give a sign. As evening drew on, hearts beat fast with anticipation, hands were full of ready gifts. There were the

tremulously expectant words of the church service, the night was past and the morning was come, the gifts were given and received, joy and peace made a flapping of wings in each heart, there was a great burst of carols, the Peace of the World had dawned, strife had passed away, every hand was linked in hand, every heart was singing.

*D. H. Lawrence*

# HURON INDIAN CAROL

'Twas in the moon of winter time when all the birds
  had fled
That Mighty Gitchi Manitou sent angel choirs instead.
Before their light the stars grew dim,
And wand'ring hunters heard the hymn;
  'Jesus, your King, is born;
  Jesus is born;
  *In Excelsis Gloria!'*

Within a lodge of broken bark the tender Babe was found.
A ragged robe of rabbit skin enwrapped His beauty round.
And as the hunter braves drew nigh,
The angel song rang loud and high:
  'Jesus, your King, is born;
  Jesus is born;
  *In Excelsis Gloria!'*

The earliest moon of winter time is not so round and fair
As was the ring of glory on the helpless Infant there.
While Chiefs from far before Him knelt,
With gifts of fox and beaver pelt.
  'Jesus, your King, is born;
  Jesus is born;
  *In Excelsis Gloria!'*

O children of the forest free, O sons of Manitou,
The Holy Child of earth and heaven is born today for you.
Come, kneel before the radiant Boy
Who brings you beauty, peace and joy.
  'Jesus, your King, is born;
  Jesus is born;
  *In Excelsis Gloria!*'

*Father Jean de Brébeuf. English interpretation by J. E. Middleton*

# Winter Landscape

In harsh weather, birds puff their feathers out to keep warmer. But in snow, or with the ground frozen, many find it hard to get food, and mortality is high in prolonged frost. When bread is thrown down, birds quickly gather, but some species are easier to help than others. Robins are tame enough to come into houses, but seem to fear the beaks of hungry starlings and woodpigeons. Blackbirds swoop down and snatch up food quicker than all other birds, though they waste time in brisk quarrels among themselves. Black-headed gulls flock in from far away and hover deftly, catching in the air any crumb that is thrown to them.

Red berries are plentiful on the holly trees, though much in demand from thrushes and blackbirds. Picking them is easier higher up, since the leaves at grazing height have prickles all round, while leaves at the top have only a single prickly point. Mistletoe flourishes in black poplars and in apple trees, though it is not so common in oaks, in spite of legend. The sticky white berries adhere to birds' bills, especially mistle thrushes', and the seeds get wiped off on the branches of other trees, which the mistletoe then colonizes. Little else is green in the bare woods and orchards, on these days when the sun stays so low.

*Derwent May*

32

All
Good Wishes
for a Happy
Xmas

MARCUS WARD & CO.    ENT. STA. HALL.

# THE BURNING BABE

As I in hoary winter's night stood shivering in the snow,
Surprised I was with sudden heat which made
my heart to glow;
And lifting up a fearful eye to view what fire was near,
A pretty Babe all burning bright did in the air appear;
Who scorched with excessive heat, such floods of tears
did shed,
As though his floods should quench his flames which
with his tears were fed.

'Alas!' quoth he, 'but newly born in fiery heats I fry,
Yet none approach to warm their hearts or feel my fire
but I.
My faultless breast the furnace is, the fuel
wounding thorns;
Love is the fire, and sighs the smoke, the ashes shame
and scorns;
The fuel justice layeth on, and mercy blows the coals;
The metal in this furnace wrought are men's defiled souls;
For which, as now on fire I am to work them to their good,
So will I melt into a bath to wash them in my blood.'
With this he vanished out of sight and swiftly
shrunk away,
And straight I called unto mind that it was Christmas day.

*Robert Southwell*

35

# Up! Good Christen Folk and Listen

Ding-dong ding, ding-a-dong-a-ding,
Ding-dong, ding-dong, ding-a-dong ding.

Up! good Christen folk, and listen
How the merry church bells ring,
And from steeple bid good people
Come adore the new born King:
Tell the story how from glory
God came down at Christmas tide,
Bringing gladness, chasing sadness,
Show'ring blessings far and wide,
Born of mother, blest o'er other,
*Ex Maria Virgine,*
In a stable ('tis no fable),
*Christus natus hodie.*

Ding-dong ding, ding-a-dong-a-ding,
Ding-dong, ding-dong, ding-a-dong ding.

*G. R. Woodward*

HARK the herald angels sing, Glory to the new-born King.

# CARDS FOR CHRISTMAS

The Christmas card is the most ubiquitous token of the festive season and it's due in large part to Sir Henry Cole who, 143 years ago, commissioned a card that was later produced for sale to the public. Before that, it was the custom for people to write 'Christmas letters' to friends. However, in 1843 (the year Charles Dickens wrote 'A Christmas Carol') Sir Henry, a founder of the Victoria and Albert Museum, left it too late to write a Yuletide message to his large circle of friends. But he was determined that his forgetfulness would not cause him to lose face, and he asked an artist friend, the future Royal Academician, John Callcott Horsley, to design for him a Christmas message that could be printed and signed.

Another friend of Sir Henry's owned a shop in London's Bond Street. He suggested that Sir Henry have a thousand cards printed so that they could be hand-tinted and sold in his shop. Sir Henry agreed, and these cards went on sale in 1846 for one shilling each.

In accord with Victorian taste, the card had an ornate design. A contemporary writer described it as 'a trellis of rustic work in the Germanesque style dividing the card into a centre and two side panels. The sides are filled with representations of the feeding of the hungry and the clothing of the naked; in the central compartment a family are shown at the table – an old man and woman, a maiden and her young man, and several children, and they are pictured drinking healths in wine.'

38

An important impetus to the custom was given by a young man with the vision to promote cards on a big scale – Adolph, son of Raphael Tuck, who sold cards in City Road, London. In 1880 he organized a nationwide competition, offering 500 guineas in prizes to seek out suitable Christmas card artists. The competition, which was judged by a panel of eminent members of the Royal Academy, attracted some 5,000 entries. It gained so much publicity that the Christmas card industry slipped into top gear. In the United States, Louis Prang and Co of Boston did much to popularize the American trade in cards, offering them from the mid-1870s.

*Mike Rice*

# MISSILES THROUGH THE POST

During the next three days about 350,000,000 Christmas cards will be fired in the British Isles. . . . The whole practice is such a thundering nuisance that it is high time that some practical advantage such as causing unhappiness was extracted out of the wretched business. I think I can point the way.

The first – and one of the most essential things to decide – is when to shoot. Timing is of critical importance. A premature Christmas card is not only ineffective but can be downright humiliating to the sender. It reveals one's position, discloses the size and weight of the ammunition and often provokes a devastating counter-attack. . . .

The next thing to understand is the value of size in Christmas cards. Important people – and people who think they are important – send big and important-looking Christmas cards. This makes the recipient feel small – which is precisely what was intended. Expensive Christmas cards can be deadly, too, for they are usually fired by expensive people to make their victims feel cheap. This is often quite costly but well worth it.

The very small Christmas card can be pretty insulting, too. Don't underestimate its destructive value. It shows what you think of the addressee – practically nothing. It is a mistake to make them too small as they then become rather cute and are liable to give pleasure. Avoid this dangerous mistake. A really contemptuous size is about

three and a half inches by two and a half inches. They are a bit difficult to obtain in the shops just now but are well worth the suffering they cause.

*Cassandra (William Connor), The Daily Mirror, 21 December 1953*

# CAROLS FOR THE
# ROYAL HORSES

Last Wednesday a choir raising money for Westminster
Children's Hospital arrived in the Royal Mews,
Buckingham Palace, to sing Christmas carols to the Royal
Household. They first sang in the courtyard of the Royal
Mews, which was alight with braziers on which chestnuts
were being roasted. Everyone gathered around a gilt and
plush throne for Father Christmas close by an illuminated
Christmas tree.

At the end of the carols, the choir were asked to proceed
to the stables. Inside the stable block they were taken to a
section where five of the Queen's greys used for State
occasions were standing quietly in their stalls.

Waiting there was the Queen – alone. She was wearing a silk headscarf, a dark green coat and leather boots. In the narrow room, barely feet away from the singers, the Queen stood by her horses whose name plates were above their stalls. All have names with Commonwealth associations. One was called 'Lusaka'.

She listened to the choir sing 'The Holly and the Ivy' and 'Good King Wenceslas'. The Queen had no special requests, saying only: 'I'll sing along with you.'

The carols over, the choir left the stable block. Led by the Queen they rejoined the festivities in the Royal Mews square where Father Christmas arrived aboard one of Queen Victoria's landaus to hand out parcels to all the children.

Amid all the merriment, the Queen quietly disappeared.

*Lady Olga Maitland, The Sunday Express, 23 December 1984*

# A SHEPHERD'S TALE

The host of heaven and the angel of the Lord had filled the sky with radiance. Now the glory of God was gone and the shepherds and the sheep stood under dim starlight. The men were shaken by the wonders they had seen and heard and, like the animals, they huddled close.

'Let us now,' said the eldest of the shepherds, 'go even unto Bethlehem, and see this thing which has come to pass, which the Lord hath made known unto us.'

The City of David lay beyond a far, high hill, upon the crest of which there danced a star. The men made haste to be away, but as they broke out of the circle there was one called Amos who remained. He dug his crook into the turf and clung to it.

'Come,' cried the eldest of the shepherds, but Amos shook his head. They marvelled, and one called out: 'It is true. It was an angel. You heard the tidings. A Saviour is born!'

'I heard,' said Amos. 'I will abide.'

The eldest walked back from the road to the little knoll on which Amos stood.

'You do not understand,' the old man told him. 'We have a sign from God. An Angel commanded us. We go to worship the Saviour, who is even now born in Bethlehem. God has made His will manifest.'

'It is not in my heart,' replied Amos.

And now the eldest of the shepherds was angry.

'With your own eyes,' he cried out, 'you have seen the

host of heaven in these dark hills. And you heard, for it was like the thunder when "Glory to God in the highest" came ringing to us out of the night.'

And again Amos said: 'It is not in my heart.'

Another shepherd then broke in. 'Because the hills still stand and the sky has not fallen, it is not enough for Amos. He must have something louder than the voice of God.'

Amos held more tightly to his crook and answered: 'I have need of a whisper.' . . . .

And when the din of the angry shepherds about him slackened, Amos pointed to his hundred.

'See my flock,' he said. 'See the fright of them. The fear of the bright angel and of the voices is still upon them. God is busy in Bethlehem. He has no time for a hundred sheep. They are my sheep. I will abide.'

This the others did not take so much amiss, for they saw that there was a terror in all the flocks and they too knew the ways of sheep. And before the shepherds departed on the road to Bethlehem towards the bright star, each talked to Amos and told him what he should do for the care of the several flocks. And yet one or two turned back a moment to taunt Amos, before they reached the dip in the road which led to the City of David. . . . . Amos paid no heed, for he thought to himself: 'One shepherd the less will not matter at the throne of God.' Nor did he have time to be troubled that he was not to see the Child

who was come to save the world. There was much to be done among the flocks and Amos walked between the sheep and made under his tongue a clucking noise, which was a way he had, and to his hundred and to the others it was a sound more fine and friendly than the voice of the bright angel. Presently the animals ceased to tremble and they began to graze as the sun came up over the hill where the stars had been.

'For sheep,' said Amos to himself, 'the angels shine too much. A shepherd is better.'

With the morning the others came up the road from Bethlehem, and they told Amos of the manger and of the wise men who had mingled there with the shepherds. And they described to him the gifts: gold, frankincense and myrrh. And when they were done they said: 'And did you see wonders here in the field with the sheep?'

Amos told them: 'Now my hundred are one hundred and one,' and he showed them a lamb which had been born just before the dawn.

'Was there for this a great voice out of heaven?' asked the eldest of the shepherds.

Amos shook his head and smiled, and there was upon his face that which seemed to the shepherds a wonder even in a night of wonders.

'To my heart,' he said, 'there came a whisper.'

*Heywood Broun*

# Xmas Day

G ood news: but if you ask me what it is, I know not;
  It is a track of feet in the snow,
  It is a lantern showing a path,
  It is a door set open.

*G. K. Chesterton*

# ACKNOWLEDGMENTS

For permission to reproduce copyright material the publishers thank the following:
The Hogarth Press for 'The Carol Singers Visit Joseph's Farm' from *Cider With Rosie*
by Laurie Lee; Oxford University Press for 'Patapan' from *The Oxford Book of Carols*;
*The New York Times* for 'Christmas in New York'; Andre Deutsch and Little, Brown and Co
for 'A Word About Winter' by Ogden Nash; The Literary Trustees of Walter de la Mare and
The Society of Authors as their representative for 'The Holly'; Viking Penguin, Inc
for 'Preparing for the Day' from *The Rainbow* by D. H. Lawrence; Robson Books Ltd for
'Winter Landscape' from *The Times Nature Diary* by Derwent May; Mike Rice;
Syndication International and Mirror Group Newspapers for 'Missiles Through the Post'
by Cassandra (William Connor); Lady Olga Maitland; Bill Cooper Associates Agency, Inc,
on behalf of Heywood Hale Broun and Patricia Broun for 'A Shepherd's Tale', originally
published under the title 'The Shepherd' in *The Collected Edition of Heywood Hale Broun*
(Harcourt Brace Jovanovich, 1941); James Flynn; Robert Kay; Katharine Fisher;
Barry Clark; Sarah Jane Porter; Helen Cornwell; Thomas Bezant; Emma Woolley;
Vicki Gilritchie and Benjamin Brown.      'Up! Good Christen Folk and Listen' is taken
from *The Cowley Carol Book* (A. R. Mowbray, 1916).      Illustrations are reproduced by
permission of The Victoria and Albert Museum; The Illustrated London News Picture
Library; Museo Civico, Forlì; Canada Post; Uffizi Gallery, Florence; American Artists Group
and The New York Public Library Picture Collection.      Original artworks were drawn by
Russell Barnett (pp19,30-31), Dennis Curran (pp29,42), Jill Moore (pp24-25) and
Julie Smith (p22).      For their help, thanks are due to Anne Glenn, Candida Twiss, and
the British Post Office Royal Mail Marketing Department.      The publishers take this
opportunity to wish all the readers of this book a very happy Christmas.